THE
DEADLIEST
CREATURE
IN THE WORLD

Brenda Z. Guiberson

Illustrated by

Gennady Spirin

Henry Holt and Company
New York

Who is the deadliest
creature in the world?

I am a **GABOON VIPER**.

I am the snake with the longest fangs and the most venom. I might be fat and slow, but I can catch birds, rodents, lizards, and even small monkeys. When I bite, a quick gush of venom stuns my prey and starts to digest my food. *That's why I am the deadliest creature in the world!*

I am an **ANOPHELES MOSQUITO.**

I bring malaria—a horrible disease that causes fever, headache, and nausea—to hundreds of millions of people. Every year, millions die after my bite. I use mouthparts to pierce skin, find blood, and pump it back to me. As a female, I need blood to develop eggs. Do you breathe? Do you move? Then I can detect you. *That's why I am the deadliest creature in the world!*

I am a **BOX JELLYFISH**.

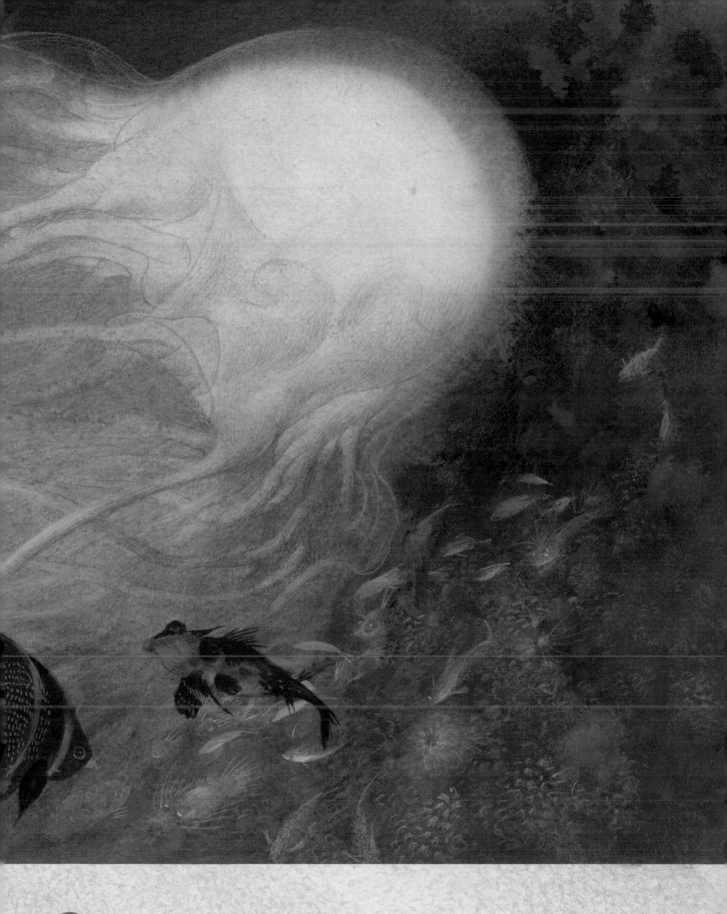

Ocean-dwellers, beware. If anything touches me, five thousand stinging cells on each of my tentacles explode with painful, heart-stopping venom. My venom acts quickly and causes intense pain. It stops prey before they can damage my soft body. *That's why I am the deadliest creature in the world!*

I am a **BRAZILIAN
WANDERING SPIDER.**

I have huge poison glands, and one bite with my fangs can affect the heart, lungs, and muscles. I like to travel and can show up anywhere. Have you checked your shoes, boxes, cars, and bananas? I hide quietly and then jump. *That's why I am the deadliest creature in the world!*

I am a **BULL SHARK**.

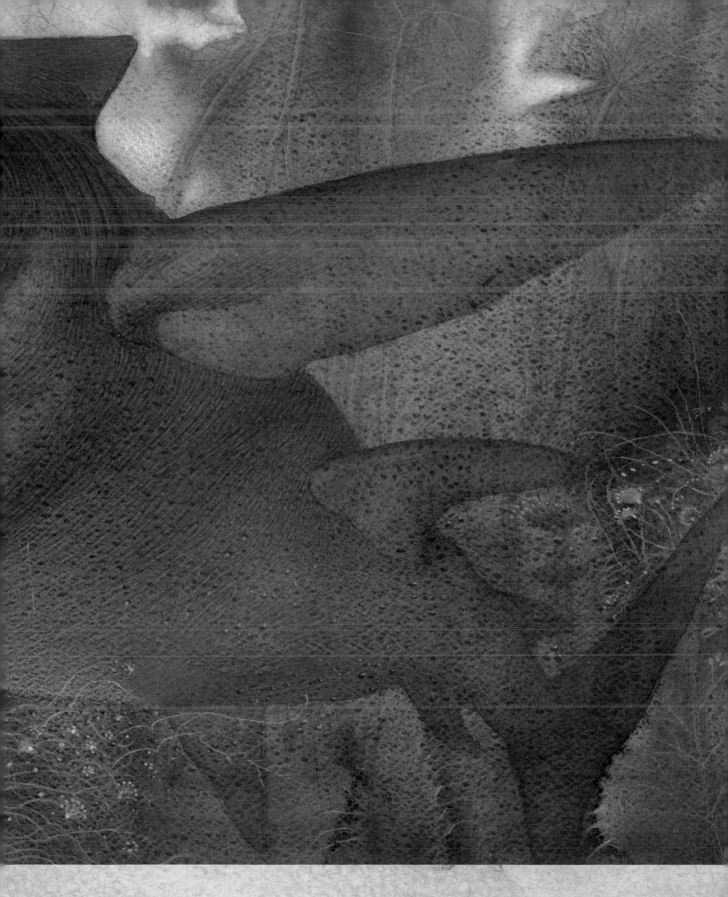

I am the shark with the strongest bite. I head-butt my prey before I attack. Like all sharks, I detect blood and electric signals from far away. Unlike other sharks, I can live in freshwater. Watch out! I can show up unexpectedly in lakes, streams, and flooded areas. *That's why I am the deadliest creature in the world!*

I am a **BLACK MAMBA.**

I am fast, fast, fast—the fastest land snake in the world, with fast-acting venom and a superfast ability to take many bites in a single second. My bite is known as the "kiss of death." Even when I am dead, my venom can kill. *That's why I am the deadliest creature in the world!*

I am a **GEOGRAPHIC CONE SNAIL.**

My potent venom contains hundreds of toxins. I can quickly change its formula for different prey. I move at a snail's pace, so I use my venom to stop victims from getting away. First I drug them into a painless sleep, and then I poison them with a chemical that causes paralysis or heart failure. *That's why I am the deadliest creature in the world!*

I am a **GOLDEN POISON DART FROG**.

I zap ants and beetles and store poison in my skin. This heart-stopping chemical transfers to anything that dares touch me. I am tiny but have enough toxin to kill ten people. I don't have to hide, because my bright color warns predators away. *That's why I am the deadliest creature in the world!*

I am a KOMODO DRAGON.

As the heaviest lizard in the world, I can weigh more than 300 pounds. I eat pig and deer and buffalo, too. I have dangling saliva that drips with venom and bacteria. My drooling bite can quickly kill, causing blood loss, shock, and infection. *That's why I am the deadliest creature in the world!*

I am an **OSTRICH**.

I am the largest bird, with massive leg muscles and a terrible four-inch claw on each foot. With the biggest eyes of all land animals, I can spot predators from two miles away. If any come near, I can kill a lion, hyena, or human with my powerful, swift kick. *That's why I am the deadliest creature in the world!*

I am a **ROCK PYTHON**.

I am the snake with the most powerful jaws. Four moving jaw parts allow me to eat an antelope three times wider than my mouth. First I coil around my victim and squeeze hard. Then I gulp and swallow while my backward-curving teeth help get my food down. *That's why I am the deadliest creature in the world!*

I am a **SHORT-TAILED SHREW.**

My saliva preserves my food. Grooves in my teeth deliver the venom, which paralyzes but doesn't kill. As a hyperactive mammal with no fat, I must eat worms, snails, insects, and mice about every two hours or I will starve. Extra bodies—alive but unable to move—are stored underground for a fresh meal later. *That's why I am the deadliest creature in the world!*

I am a SMASHER MANTIS SHRIMP.

I have the strongest punch. My spring-loaded forearms thrust out at fifty miles per hour to smash open shells. I can even break glass. With the most complex eyes in the animal kingdom, I am able to see multiple colors and lights. Little can hide from me—not even transparent shrimp. *That's why I am the deadliest creature in the world!*

I am a STONEFISH.

I am the fish with the most venom. I may look lumpy and ragged, but this is my camouflage. I lie in wait for my food. If something touches me, my spiky spines deliver a painful blast of venom that causes shock, paralysis, and tissue death. *That's why I am the deadliest creature in the world!*

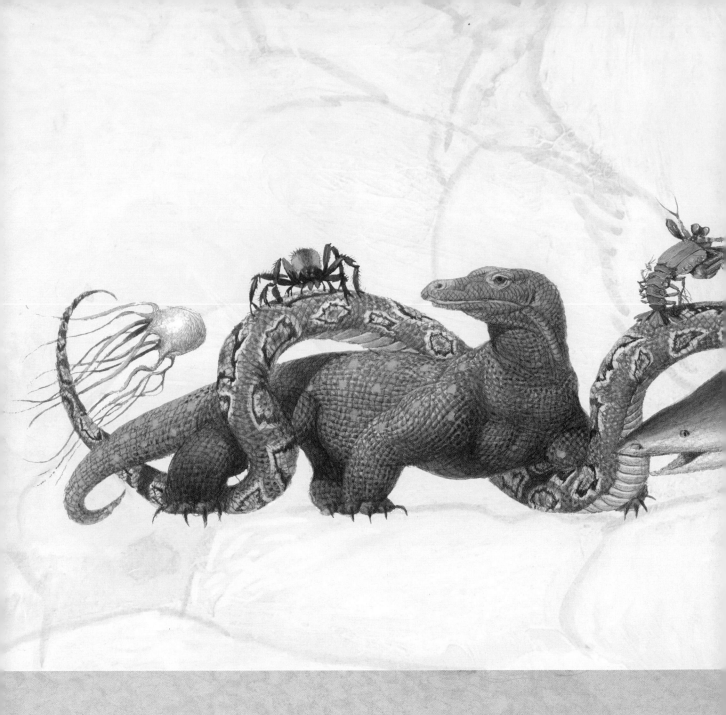

Every creature needs to eat and defend itself.

Sometimes a swift kick, a smashing punch, or a powerful bite will do the trick. But what about creatures that are fragile or teensy or slow? What about the ones with no arms or legs? They have been surviving for hundreds of millions of years with the help of toxins and poisons. With eons to fine-tune their formulas, they ooze with natural concoctions that affect the heart, nerves, muscles, blood, lungs, digestion, pain, brains, and sleep.

So who is the deadliest creature?

Is it the one with the longest fangs, the deadly disease, the most overpowering venom, huge poison glands, the strongest bite, the fastest bite, a quick-change formula, or the one who stores poison? Or maybe it is the one with dangling saliva, a superpower kick, the widest gaping jaws, saliva that preserves victims, the strongest punch, or the most venom.

Don't come too close while you ponder and decide.

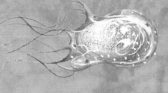

For Grandpa Bill and little PJ,
with the greatest spunk,
grandest charm, and strongest resilience
—B. Z. G.

To my grandson Nikolai
—G. S.

With thanks to Laura Godwin, Julia Sooy, and Patrick Collins
for their inspired and creative work on this book.
—B. Z. G.

Henry Holt and Company, LLC
Publishers since 1866
175 Fifth Avenue
New York, New York 10010
mackids.com

Henry Holt® is a registered trademark of Henry Holt and Company, LLC.
Text copyright © 2016 by Brenda Z. Guiberson
Illustrations copyright © 2016 by Gennady Spirin
All rights reserved.

Library of Congress Cataloging-in-Publication Data
Guiberson, Brenda Z.
The deadliest creature in the world / Brenda Z. Guiberson,
Gennady Spirin.—First edition.
pages   cm
Audience: Ages 4 to 8.
ISBN 978-1-62779-198-4 (hardcover)
1. Dangerous animals—Juvenile literature. I. Spirin, Gennady. II. Title.
QL100.G85 2016   591.6'5—dc23   2015015541

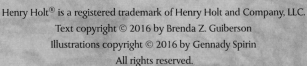
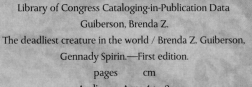

Our books may be purchased in bulk for promotional, educational, or business use.
Please contact your local bookseller or the Macmillan Corporate and Premium Sales Department
at (800) 221-7945 ext. 5442 or by e-mail at MacmillanSpecialMarkets@macmillan.com.

First Edition—2016 / Designed by Patrick Collins
The artist used tempera, watercolor, and pencil on Arches watercolor paper to create the illustrations for this book.
Printed in China by RR Donnelley Asia Printing Solutions Ltd., Dongguan City, Guangdong Province

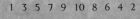

1 3 5 7 9 10 8 6 4 2